## MATH SMARTS!

# Geometry

## SMARTS!

Lucille Caron
Philip M. St. Jacques

**Enslow Publishers, Inc.**
40 Industrial Road
Box 398
Berkeley Heights, NJ 07922
USA

http://www.enslow.com

Original edition published as *Geometry* in 2001.

**Library of Congress Cataloging-in-Publication Data**

Caron, Lucille.
  Geometry smarts! / Lucille Caron and Philip M. St. Jacques.
     p. cm. — (Math smarts!)
  Summary: "Re-inforce classroom learning of geometry skills such as points, lines, planes, triangles, circles, quadrilaterals, perimeter, area, and circumference"—Provided by publisher.
  Includes index.
  ISBN 978-0-7660-3935-3
  1.  Geometry—Juvenile literature.  I. St. Jacques, Philip M. II. Title.
  QA445.5.C373 2012
  516—dc22

                                                                          2011008384

Paperback ISBN: 978-1-59845-316-4

Printed in China

052011 Leo Paper Group, Heshan City, Guangdong, China

10 9 8 7 6 5 4 3 2 1

**To Our Readers:** We have done our best to make sure all Internet addresses in this book were active and appropriate when we went to press. However, the author and the publisher have no control over and assume no liability for the material available on those Internet sites or on other Web sites they may link to. Any comments or suggestions can be sent by e-mail to comments@enslow.com or to the address on the back cover.

**Cover Illustration:** Shutterstock.com

# Contents

# Introduction

If you were to look up the meaning of the word *mathematics*, you would find that it is the study of numbers, quantities, and shapes, and how they relate to each other.

Mathematics is very important to all world cultures, including our world of work. The following are just some of the ways in which studying math will help you:

▶ You will know how much money you are spending at the store and if the cashier has given you the right change.

▶ You will know how to use measurements to build things.

▶ Your science classes will be easier and more interesting.

▶ You will understand music on a whole new level.

▶ You will be empowered to qualify for and land a rewarding job.

*Geometry* comes from the Greek word *geometria* and means "earth measure." It means you can use geometry to measure anything on earth. No matter what shape something has, you can measure its perimeter and area or volume. And no matter what size a rectangle is—whether it be a computer chip, an Olympic-sized swimming pool, or a city block—you can always find its area by multiplying length by width.

How does a builder know how big a roof will be on a new house? Geometry! How does a gardener know how many bags of fertilizer will cover the garden? Geometry! How do we know how much water is in the ocean? Geometry!

This book has been written so that you can learn about geometry at your own speed. Use it on your own or with a friend, tutor, or parent.

*Good luck and have fun!*

Some important terms that are frequently used in geometry are Point, Line, and Plane.

## Point

A point has position and it determines a location in space. The symbol for a point is a dot (·). It can be written as "Ä" and read as "point A."

## Line

In geometry, a line extends endlessly in both directions. It is a continuous set of points in a straight path that goes on forever.

A line is named by any two points that lie on it. The symbol for a line is an arrow ←——————→.

Lines can be horizontal, vertical, or oblique.

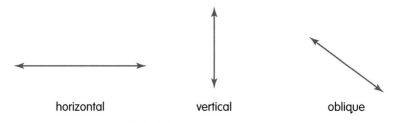

horizontal           vertical           oblique

The line below can be called CE, EC, or line L. The first two names are read "line CE" and "line EC."

←————•————•————→ L
        C     E

There is an infinite number of points on any **line**.
Two points determine one **line**.

## Plane

A plane is any flat surface that continues in all directions. You can think of a plane as a flat table top that extends forever in all directions. A plane is named by any three points that lie on it. The plane below is named as plane XYZ.

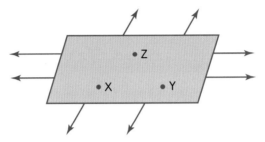

## Intersecting Lines

Two lines that meet are called intersecting lines.

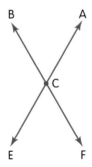

$\overleftrightarrow{BF}$ intersects $\overleftrightarrow{AE}$ at point C.

This is read as "line BF intersects line AE at point C."

Two intersecting straight lines will meet at one **point**.
Three points, not all on a straight line, determine a **plane**.

## Line Segment

A line segment is part of a line. It has two endpoints.

The symbol for a line segment is ——. The line segment above is written as $\overline{FG}$ or $\overline{GF}$ and read "line segment FG" or "line segment GF."

The shortest distance between two points is a line segment.

## Ray

A ray is part of a line. It has one endpoint but goes on forever in the other direction. Two examples are

The symbol for a ray is an arrow in one direction: ⟶ or ⟵. The above are written as $\overrightarrow{XY}$ and $\overleftarrow{AB}$ and read, "ray XY" and "ray BA."

To name a ray, name the endpoint and any other point on the ray. The first letter used in naming a ray is always the endpoint.

You can think of a **ray** as a ray of sunshine that starts at the sun and continues on forever. The endpoint is the sun.

## Perpendicular Lines

Two lines that intersect and form a right angle are called perpendicular lines. A right angle measures 90 degrees. You will learn more about angles on pages 10–11.

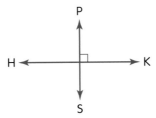

Line PS is perpendicular to line HK. The symbol for perpendicular is ⊥. We write this as $\overset{\leftrightarrow}{PS} \perp \overset{\leftrightarrow}{HK}$.

## Parallel Lines

Parallel lines are two lines that lie in the same plane yet never intersect. The shortest distance between parallel lines is the same along the entire length of the lines.

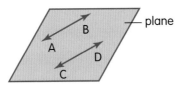

Line AB is parallel to line CD. The symbol for parallel is ||. We write this as $\overset{\leftrightarrow}{AB} \parallel \overset{\leftrightarrow}{CD}$.

## Skewed Lines

Lines that are not in the same plane and do not intersect are called skewed lines. Lines KL and RT are skewed lines.

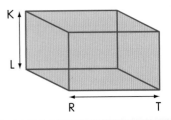

Rays or segments are parallel if the lines that contain them are parallel.

Angles are formed whenever two lines intersect. They can be measured using a protractor. Navigators use a different tool, a sextant, to measure the angle between the horizon and the sun. It helps them determine their exact location on Earth.

## Definition of an Angle

An angle is made when two lines intersect or two rays share one endpoint. The point of intersection or the endpoint is called the angle's vertex.

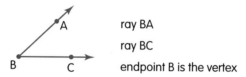

ray BA

ray BC

endpoint B is the vertex

The symbol for an angle is ∠. The above angle is written as ∠B. It can also be written as ∠ABC or ∠CBA.

## Classification of Angles

Angles are classified according to their size. They are measured in units called degrees (°).

**Right Angle**

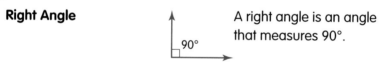

A right angle is an angle that measures 90°.

When two lines or rays form a right angle, they are said to be perpendicular.

**Straight Angle**

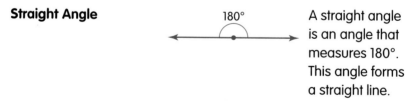

A straight angle is an angle that measures 180°. This angle forms a straight line.

When you write an angle with three letters, the **vertex** is always the middle letter. For example, in ∠ABC, B is the vertex of the angle.

**Acute Angle**

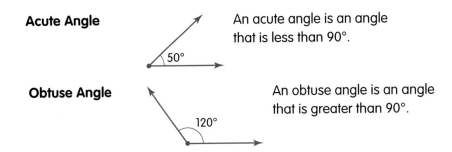

An acute angle is an angle that is less than 90°.

**Obtuse Angle**

An obtuse angle is an angle that is greater than 90°.

## Pairs of Angles

Pairs of angles are related. Look at the following pairs of angles:

### Complementary Angles

Two angles are complementary if their measures have a sum of 90°.

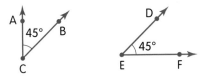

∠ACB and ∠DEF are complementary angles. The sum of the two angles is equal to 90° (45° + 45° = 90°).

### Supplementary Angles

Two angles are supplementary if their measures have a sum of 180°.

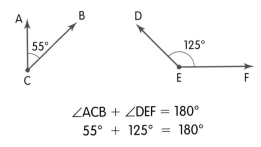

$$\angle ACB + \angle DEF = 180°$$
$$55° + 125° = 180°$$

---

**complementary angles** — Two angles whose measures add up to 90°.
**supplementary angles** — Two angles whose measures add up to 180°.

A polygon is a closed plane figure that is bounded by line segments. Each of these line segments is called a side.

There are three things that must be true of a figure for it to be a polygon:

1. The figure must be closed.

closed — polygon          not closed — not a polygon

2. The figure must be bounded by line segments. A circle is not a polygon because it is not bounded by line segments (straight lines).

polygon          not a polygon

3. The figure must lie in one plane.

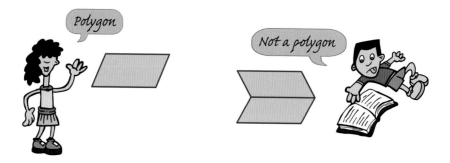

Polygon          Not a polygon

What different types of polygons do you see everyday? For example, where do you see triangles, rectangles, or octagons?

**polygon** — A shape in one plane that is bounded by line segments.

## Classification of Polygons

Polygons are classified by the number of sides or angles they have. Look at the following table.

| Polygons | Sides | Angles |
|---|---|---|
| Triangle | 3 | 3 |
| Quadrilateral | 4 | 4 |
| Pentagon | 5 | 5 |
| Hexagon | 6 | 6 |
| Octagon | 8 | 8 |
| Nanogon | 9 | 9 |
| Decagon | 10 | 10 |

Notice that the lengths of the sides or the sizes of the angles do not determine a polygon's class.

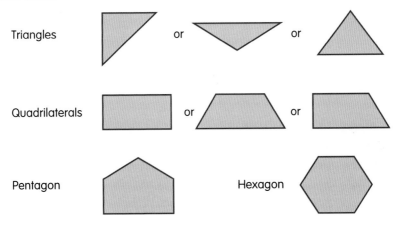

Triangles ... or ... or

Quadrilaterals ... or ... or

Pentagon

Hexagon

Look at shapes of road signs with a friend or family member. Make a list of the road signs and classify them according to the number of their sides. For example, a yield sign has three sides: it is a triangle.

The four angles in a **quadrilateral** add up to 360°.

A triangle is a three-sided polygon. Triangles have three line segments for sides and three angles. You can name a triangle by listing the vertices of the angles in any way you choose. The symbol for a triangle is△.

Name the triangle.

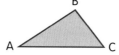

There are six ways to name this triangle:

△BAC or △CAB, △CBA    △ABC, △BCA or △ACB.

Name the three sides of the triangle.
**side 1:** $\overline{CB}$ or $\overline{BC}$    **side 2:** $\overline{CA}$ or $\overline{AC}$    **side 3:** $\overline{AB}$ or $\overline{BA}$

## Classification of Triangles by Lengths of Sides

You can classify triangles by the lengths of their sides and therefore the relative sizes of their angles.

### Equilateral Triangle

An equilateral triangle is a triangle that has all sides equal in length. The triangles also have all angles equal in measure.

The word *congruent* is used in geometry when line segments or angles have equal measures. You can use a hatch mark to indicate which sides or angles of a triangle are congruent.

$$\overline{AB} = \overline{BC} = \overline{CA}$$

$$\angle B = \angle A = \angle C$$

Two figures are **congruent** if they are the same size and same shape.
All the angles of a triangle add up to 180°.

## Isosceles Triangle

An isosceles triangle has two congruent (equal) sides and two congruent angles.

The sides opposite congruent angles are congruent sides.

## Scalene Triangle

A scalene triangle has no congruent sides and no congruent angles.

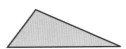

# Classification of Triangles by Angles

You can also classify triangles by the measure of their angles. The sum of the measures of the angles in any triangle is 180°.

## Right Triangle

A right triangle contains one right angle.

The sum of the measures of a right triangle is 180°. In this example, the angles are 90°, 60°, and 30°.

$$90° + 60° + 30° = 180°$$

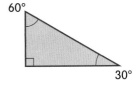

## Acute Triangle

An acute triangle contains three acute angles. Each angle in an acute triangle is less than 90°, but they all still add up to 180°.
For example: 40° + 60° + 80° = 180°.

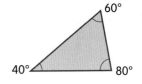

## Obtuse Triangle

An obtuse triangle has one angle greater than 90° and two angles that add up to less than 90°.
For example: 110° + 50° + 20° = 180°.

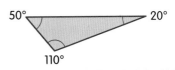

---

**acute angle** — An angle less than 90°.
**obtuse angle** — An angle greater than 90°.
**right angle** — An angle equal to 90°.

A circle is a plane figure bounded by one curved line. All points that lie on that boundary must be an equal distance from a fixed point on the plane called the center. You can draw a circle by using an instrument called a compass.

## Circumference

The length of the boundary of a circle is called the circumference of the circle. The circumference of a circle is another name for the perimeter of a circle.

## Radius

The radius of a circle is a line segment that has one endpoint on the circle and one endpoint at the center of the circle.

**radius** $= \overline{BA}$

## Chord

A chord is a line segment that connects any two points on the circle.

**chord** $= \overline{DC}$

## Diameter

The diameter of a circle is a chord that passes through the center of the circle. It is the longest chord possible for that circle.

**diameter** $= \overline{DE}$

A **chord** that passes through the center of a circle is called a **diameter**.

## Central Angles

A central angle has the center of a circle as its vertex.

| | |
|---|---|
| **central angle** | ∠DAC or ∠CAD |
| **Also,** | ∠SAD, ∠DAQ, |
| | ∠QAR, ∠SAR, ∠CAQ, |
| | ∠CAR, ∠CAS |

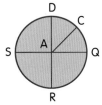

## Semicircle

A semicircle is a half circle. It is named by three points on its circumference.

semicircle DAB

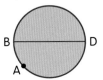

## Arc

An arc is part of a circle named by either two or three points on the circumference of a circle. If an arc is less than half the circle, it is called a minor arc and is named by two points on the circumference.

minor arc CD

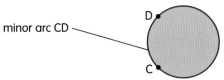

A major arc is equal to or greater than half a circle and is named by three points.

*The major arc is GEF.*

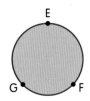

---

**minor arc** — An arc on a circle that is less than half the circle.
**major arc** — An arc on a circle that is half or more than half the circle.

A quadrilateral is a polygon with four sides. There are different types of quadrilaterals, such as trapezoids, parallelograms, rhombuses, rectangles, and squares.

## Trapezoids

A trapezoid is a quadrilateral that has one pair of opposite sides that are parallel. The figures below are examples of trapezoids.

## Parallelograms

A parallelogram is a quadrilateral that has two pairs of opposite sides that are parallel. Squares, rectangles, and rhombuses are special types of parallelograms.

 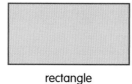 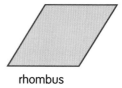

square          rectangle          rhombus

Each of these quadrilaterals has two pairs of opposite sides that are parallel.

**Remember:** Parallel lines are lines that never meet.
**parallelogram** — Quadrilaterals with opposite sides that are parallel.

## Rhombus

A rhombus is a parallelogram because it has two sets of parallel sides. In addition, it has four congruent sides.

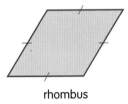

rhombus

## Rectangle

A rectangle is also a parallelogram because it has two sets of parallel sides. In addition, it has four right angles.

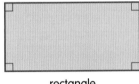

rectangle

## Square

A square is a parallelogram with four right angles and four equal sides. A square is both a rectangle and a rhombus.

Check it out.

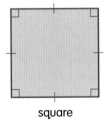

square

List all the places where you see examples of quadrilaterals.

Every **rectangle** is a parallelogram.
Every **rhombus** is a parallelogram.
Every **square** is a rectangle, a rhombus, and a parallelogram.

Polygons are two-dimensional. That means they have only length and width.

A prism is a three-dimensional figure. It has length, width, and height.

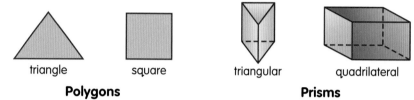

| triangle | square | triangular | quadrilateral |

**Polygons**          **Prisms**

Prisms are named by their bases. The bases must be polygons. There are several parts of a prism: *face, edge, vertex,* and *base.*

## Face

A face is a side of a three-dimensional figure. Faces:

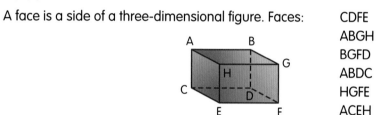

CDFE
ABGH
BGFD
ABDC
HGFE
ACEH

This quadrilateral prism has six faces.

## Edge

An edge is a line segment that connects two faces. The figure above has 12 edges: $\overline{AC}$, $\overline{AB}$, $\overline{BD}$, $\overline{CD}$, $\overline{BG}$, $\overline{GF}$, $\overline{DF}$, $\overline{HG}$, $\overline{EF}$, $\overline{CE}$, $\overline{HE}$, and $\overline{AH}$.

## Vertex

The point formed by the intersection of three edges or three faces is called a vertex. In the figure above there are 8 vertices: A, B, C, D, E, F, G, and H.

**Two-dimensional objects** have length and width.
**Three-dimensional objects** have length, width, and height.

## Base

Two faces of a prism are called bases if they lie in parallel planes and are the same size and shape. In the figure on page 20, ABGH and CDFE are bases, ACEH and BDFG are bases, and ABDC and HGFE are bases.

## Naming Prisms

Prisms are named by the shape of their bases.

A quadrilateral prism has bases that are squares or rectangles.
A triangular prism has bases that are triangles.
A pentagonal prism has bases that are pentagons.
A hexagonal prism has bases that are hexagons.

The table below lists different kinds of prisms.

| Name of Prism | Number of Faces | Number of Edges | Number of Vertices |
|---|---|---|---|
| Triangular | 5 | 9 | 6 |
| Quadrilateral | 6 | 12 | 8 |
| Pentagonal | 7 | 15 | 10 |
| Hexagonal | 8 | 18 | 12 |
| Heptagonal | 9 | 21 | 14 |
| Octagonal | 10 | 24 | 16 |

That's cool.

An **angle** is a figure formed by two rays with the same endpoint. The endpoint is called the **vertex**.

Giant pyramids were built by the ancient Egyptians to serve as tombs. A pyramid has a polygon for its base and triangular sides that meet at a common point. Pyramids are named by the shape of their base. The pyramid below is called a quadrilateral pyramid because the base of the pyramid is a quadrilateral.

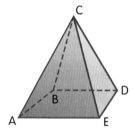

## Base
ABDE is called the base of the pyramid.

## Lateral Faces
The triangular surfaces CAB, CBD, CED, and CAE are called lateral faces of the pyramid.

## Faces
The base and lateral faces are all faces of a pyramid. The faces of the pyramid are ABDE, CAB, CBD, CED, and CAE.

## Edges
As you learned, an edge is a line segment formed by the intersection of two faces.

$$\overline{AB}, \overline{AC}, \overline{BD}, \overline{BC}, \overline{CE}, \overline{ED}, \overline{CD}, \text{ and } \overline{AE} \text{ are edges.}$$

The point at which the faces of a pyramid meet is called the **vertex**.

## Vertices

The point formed by the intersection of three edges or three faces is called the vertex. A, B, C, D, and E are all vertices.

## Naming Pyramids

Just like prisms, pyramids are named according to the polygonal region that forms the base. A quadrilateral pyramid has a base that is formed by a square or rectangle. A triangular pyramid has a base that is formed by a triangle. A pentagonal pyramid has a base that is formed by a pentagon. A hexagonal pyramid has a base that is formed by a hexagon. The list below contains information on different kinds of pyramids.

| Name of Pyramid | Number of Faces | Number of Edges | Number of Vertices |
|---|---|---|---|
| Triangular | 4 | 6 | 4 |
| Quadrilateral | 5 | 8 | 5 |
| Pentagonal | 6 | 10 | 6 |
| Hexagonal | 7 | 12 | 7 |
| Heptagonal | 8 | 14 | 8 |
| Octagonal | 9 | 16 | 9 |

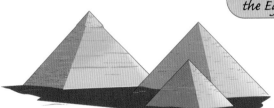

What types of pyramids did the Egyptians build?

Pyramids are classified by the shape of their bases: triangular, square, rectangular, and hexagonal, for example.

# 10 Congruent Figures

If you have ever made a copy of your house key, then you have made a congruent figure. The copy of the key should open your door since it is the same shape and size as the first key. Congruent figures are figures that have the same shape and size.

**Congruent figures**

Are the three figures below congruent?

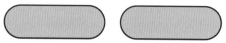

These shapes are not the same. They do not have the same size or shape, so they are not congruent.

## Symbols

The symbol ≅ is used to compare congruent figures and is read as "is congruent to."

$$\overline{AB} \cong \overline{CD}$$

Line segment AB is congruent to line segment CD. Hatch marks ( | ) are used to show which lines are congruent.

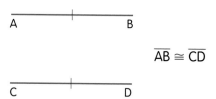

Two segments are **congruent** if they have the same length.

## Corresponding Sides

Two figures are congruent if one figure can fit exactly on the other. The sides that match each other are called corresponding sides.

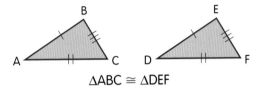

**corresponding sides**

AB ≅ DE

AC ≅ DF

BC ≅ EF

$\triangle ABC \cong \triangle DEF$

Triangle ABC is congruent to triangle DEF because the corresponding sides are congruent. The triangles have the same size and shape.

## Corresponding Angles

Two triangles are congruent if the corresponding angles and the corresponding sides are congruent.

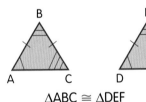

**corresponding angles**

∠A ≅ ∠D

∠B ≅ ∠E

∠C ≅ ∠F

$\triangle ABC \cong \triangle DEF$

Triangle ABC is congruent to triangle DEF because the corresponding angles are congruent and the corresponding sides are congruent.

Name three items in your house that are congruent. Do your family members agree with the items you selected?

Two triangles are **congruent** when all corresponding angles and all corresponding sides are equal.

Similar figures are figures that have the same shape but not necessarily the same size. One way they are used is for drawing or building models. You can think of a figure being similar to another if one is an enlargement or reduction of the other.

## Similar Triangles

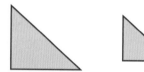

These triangles have the same shape but they are not the same size. The symbol ~ is used to compare similar figures and is read as "is similar to."

## Corresponding Angles

Corresponding angles of similar triangles are congruent.

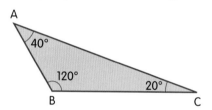 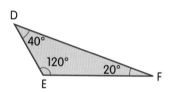

The corresponding angles have the same measurement, in degrees.

**Corresponding Angles**

$\angle A \cong \angle D$

$\angle B \cong \angle E$

$\angle C \cong \angle F$

The triangles are similar. △ABC ~ △DEF

---

The **symbol** ~ is read as "is similar to."

## Ratios of Corresponding Sides

Triangles are similar if the corresponding angles are equal. As a result, the ratios of the lengths of corresponding sides are also equal. Let's look at the corresponding sides of these two triangles. The symbol for *corresponds to* is ↔.

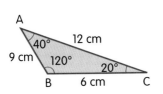 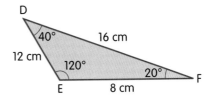

### Corresponding sides

$$\overline{AB} \leftrightarrow \overline{DE}$$
$$\overline{BC} \leftrightarrow \overline{EF}$$
$$\overline{AC} \leftrightarrow \overline{DF}$$

You can compare the sides of similar triangles by using ratios.

$$\frac{\text{length } \overline{AB}}{\text{length } \overline{DE}} = \frac{9}{12} = \frac{9 \div 3}{12 \div 3} = \frac{3}{4}$$

$$\frac{\text{length } \overline{BC}}{\text{length } \overline{EF}} = \frac{6}{8} = \frac{3}{4}$$

$$\frac{\text{length } \overline{AC}}{\text{length } \overline{DF}} = \frac{12}{16} = \frac{3}{4}$$

△ABC ~ △DEF because the corresponding angles are congruent. The ratios of the lengths of corresponding sides are equal.

Two geometric figures are **similar** if they have the same shape but generally not the same size.

**ratio** — A comparison of two quantities.

Many designers use symmetry to create their designs and to create two matching parts. Some buildings are designed to be symmetrical.

You can create a line of symmetry in the drawing of the house below by placing a line down the center of the house. The house has two matching halves.

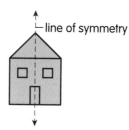

## One Line of Symmetry

The word *symmetrical* means "having the same measure." A figure is symmetrical if its two halves are the same size and shape. To find out if a figure is symmetrical, fold it to see if both halves match. The fold line is called the line of symmetry. If both sides match, then the figure has a line of symmetry.

The figure below has one line of symmetry.

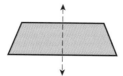

If you fold the above figure along that line, it would look like the one below.

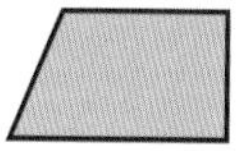

It has only one line of symmetry because there is no other fold line that would make both halves identical.

The exterior of your body is **symmetrical**. The right half is a mirror image of the left half.

## Two or More Lines of Symmetry

Some figures have more than one line of symmetry. All lines of symmetry divide a figure into two equal, or congruent, parts.

An equilateral triangle (a triangle with three equal sides) has three lines of symmetry, but an isosceles triangle has only one.

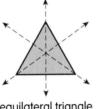 

equilateral triangle          isosceles triangle

A square has four lines of symmetry.

A rectangle has two lines of symmetry.

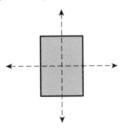

Try to think of items or figures that have one or more lines of symmetry. Don't forget numbers and letters of the alphabet. For example, the number 3 has one line of symmetry: ←3→

**Symmetry** is the balance that a shape has.

Square numbers can be represented by square arrays of dots. An array is an orderly arrangement in rows and columns. The numbers 4, 9, and 16 are examples of square numbers.

Draw an array for 4.

$2 \times 2$

The square of 2 is 4.

$$2 \times 2 = 4$$

Therefore, stack two circles above 2 circles to make the square array.

Draw an array for 9.

$3 \times 3$

Draw an array for 16.

$4 \times 4$

*That's good to know.*

---

**array** — An orderly arrangement in rows and columns.

The numbers 3, 6, and 10 are examples of triangular numbers. These numbers can be represented by triangular arrays of dots.

Draw an array for 3 in the shape of a right triangle.

Draw an array for 6.

Draw an array for 10.

Draw an array for 15.

Some numbers are both triangular and square. The number 36 can be represented by a triangular array or a square array.

Triangular array for 36

Rectangular array for 36

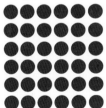

**square numbers** — A number represented by a square array of dots.
**triangular numbers** — A number represented by a triangular array of dots.

Do you have a bookcase in your house? How many rectangles can you find in the bookcase?

How many rectangles do you see in this figure?

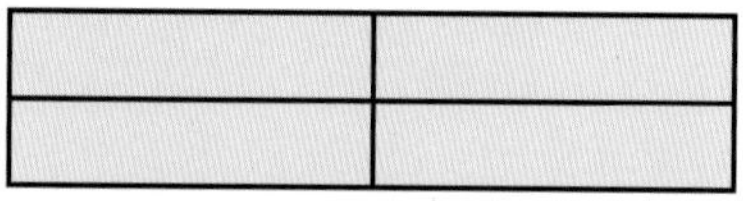

To find all the rectangles, label each section of the figure.

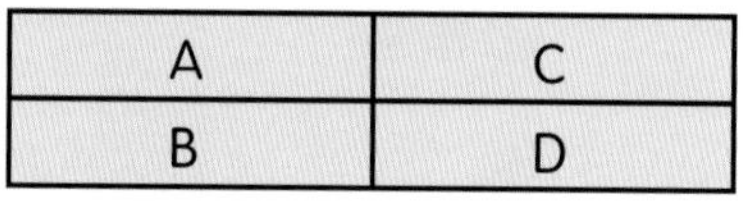

| A | C |
| B | D |

There are 4 one-section rectangles.

| A | | C |
| B | | D |

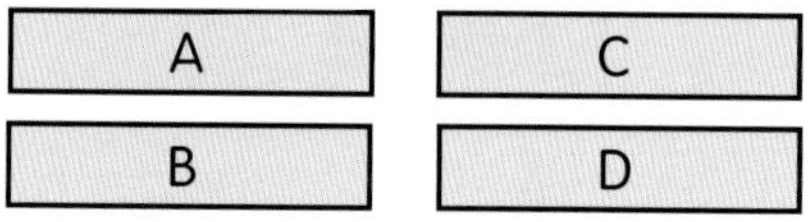

There are 4 two-section rectangles.

| A | C |
| B | D |

| A |
| B |

| C |
| D |

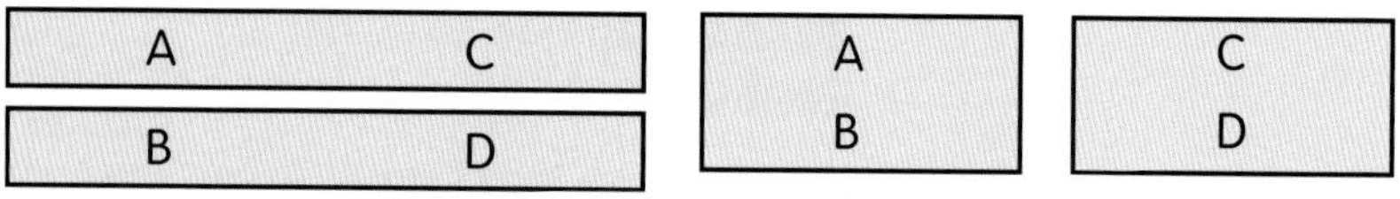

There is 1 four-section rectangle.

| A | C |
| B | D |

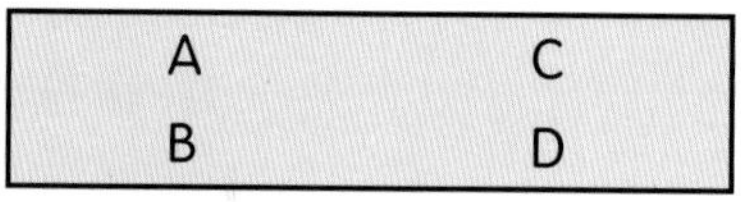

To find the total, add all the rectangles.

$$\begin{array}{r} 4 \text{ one-section rectangles} \\ 4 \text{ two-section rectangles} \\ + 1 \text{ four-section rectangle} \end{array}$$

There are 9 rectangles in the figure.

Carpenters use many geometric facts when building bookcases. Can you name at least one fact they use?

How many triangles are in the following figure?

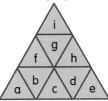

There are 9 one-section triangles.

There are 3 four-section triangles.

There is 1 nine-section triangle.

To find the total, add all the triangles.

9 one-section triangles
3 four-section triangles
+ 1 nine-section triangle
13

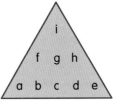

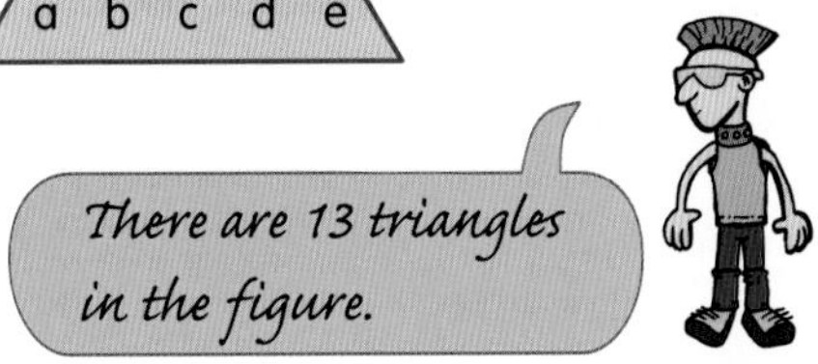

There are 13 triangles in the figure.

Count the number of rectangles in your bookcase. How many did you find?

## Cones and Cylinders

A cone is a three-dimensional figure that has a closed curve for a base. This type of base is called a nonpolygon. (Remember, a polygon is bounded by line segments.) The surface of a cone comes to a point, called the vertex. An ice cream cone is an example of a cone.

polygonal base                                    nonpolygonal base

A cone has a base, a vertex, and a lateral face.

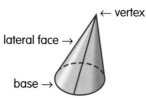

← vertex

lateral face →

base →

## Circular Cone

A cone that has a circular base is called a circular cone.

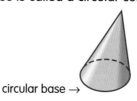

circular base →

## Right Circular Cone

In a right circular cone, the line segment that joins the vertex with the center of the base is perpendicular to the base.

To review polygons and nonpolygons, see pages 12–13.

**vertex** — The point of a cone.

## Cylinder

A can is an example of a cylinder. A cylinder is a figure in space that has two parallel bases. The bases are congruent nonpolygons.

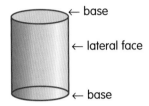

← base

← lateral face

← base

It also has a curved surface. It has no vertex. The lateral face is the surface that joins the bases.

## Right Cylinder

If the line segment joining the center of the two bases is parallel to the sides and perpendicular to the bases, then the cylinder is called a right cylinder.

A cylinder that has two circular bases is called a circular cylinder. The shape of the bases, not the shape of the faces, names a space figure.

Think of some items that are in the shape of a cone or cylinder. Which ones are right cylinders?

Remember, **congruent** means having the same size and shape.

Figures look different when they are seen from different positions. In geometry, you will need to know how to imagine shapes in different positions.

Look at the top, front, and side views of the figure below. What is it?

| Top | Front | Side | Bottom |
|-----|-------|------|--------|

If you guessed a cone, you were correct.

Draw the top, front, and side views of the table below.

## Top View
Look down at the table. What does it look like from the top?

The table top looks like a rectangle. Draw a rectangle.

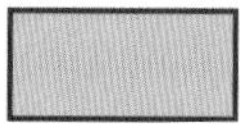

## Front View
Look at the front of the table at eye-level. Draw what you see.

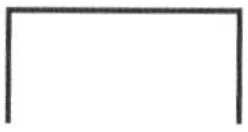

## Side View
Look at the side of the table. Draw what you see.

Draw the top, front, and side views of your mathematics textbook.

Look at the top, front, and side views of the figure below.

| Top | Front | Side | Bottom |
|---|---|---|---|
|  |  |  |  |

What is it? If you said a mug, you were correct.

Find a can of soup in your kitchen cabinet. Place it on your kitchen table. Draw the top, front, and side views of the can.

## Top View
Look down at the can. What does it look like from the top?

## Front View
Hold the can in front of you. Draw what you see.

## Side View
Place the can back on the table. Look at it from the side. What do you see?

The side and front views of the can are the same. The can is an example of a right cylinder.

Draw the top, front, and side views of another figure or item. Show it to a friend. Can he or she name the figure or item you drew?

Architects use isometric drawings to show different views of whatever they are building. The views are all of the same scale: **Isometrics** means "with equal measure."

A slide is made by moving a figure or object along a line.

Look at the figure below. Then you can create an identical figure to one that exists. This is an important skill to learn in geometry.

Look at the figure below.

To draw the slide image, first draw a line under the figure and call it L. Place a dot on the line.

Draw the same figure where the dot is located.

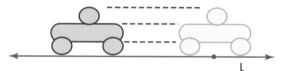

This image is called a slide image. It is the same as the original figure, but in a different location on the line.

To draw the slide image of the letter B, draw a line under the letter. Place a dot on the line.

Draw the slide image where the dot is located.

**Slides** are also called **translations**. Every point of the object you are sliding, or translating, moves the same distance and the same direction along a line.

Slides move figures along a horizontal or vertical line without changing the way it looks.

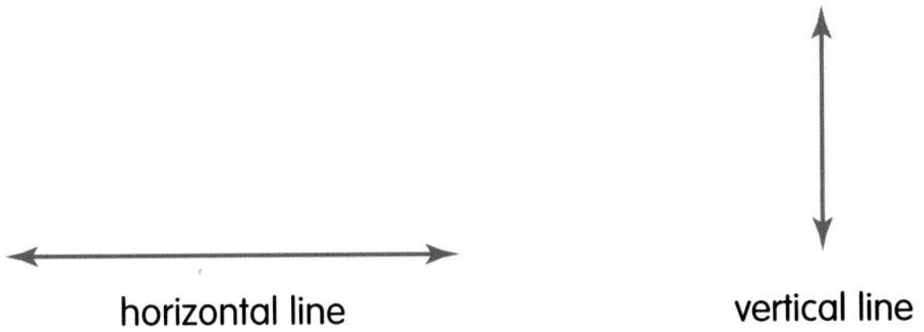

horizontal line

vertical line

Draw the slide image of the figure below.

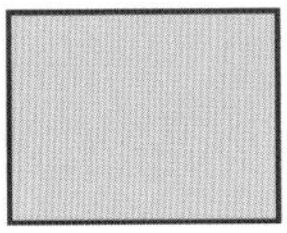

Draw a vertical line. Place a dot on the line.

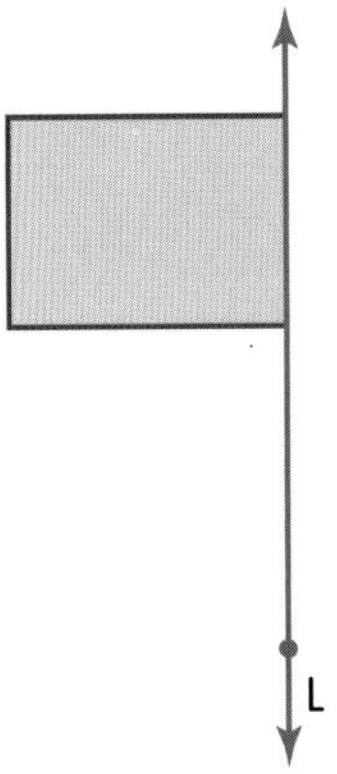

L

Draw the same image on the dot.

*I can do this!*

L

Some figures are difficult to draw. You can use carbon paper to trace the image.

A flip image is called a reflection. It is made by creating a line of symmetry. The line of symmetry will divide the final figure into two congruent halves. The congruent halves will be reflections, or mirror images, of each other.

Draw the reflection of the triangle, ABC.

**Step 1:** Draw a line of symmetry and call it L.

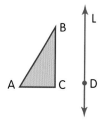

**Step 2:** Draw a line segment from C to D. Extend the segment to C' so that the line segment CD is congruent to line segment DC':

$$\overline{CD} \cong \overline{DC'}.$$

**Step 3:** Repeat this procedure for vertices A and B. Connect A', B', and C'.

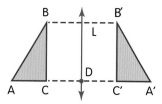

This new image is called the reflection of the original triangle.

---

**Reflection** is a way of transforming a shape as a mirror does.

Draw the reflection of the figure below.

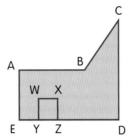

**Step 1:** Draw a line of symmetry and call it L. Draw a line segment from D to F. Extend the segment to D' so that line segment DF is congruent to line segment FD'. $\overline{DF} \cong \overline{FD'}$

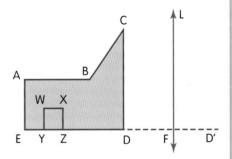

**Step 2:** Repeat this procedure for C, B, A, and E, and for W, X, Y, and Z.

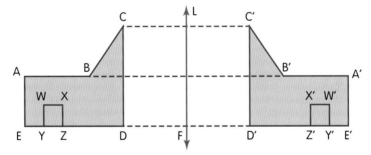

Compare the image with the original figure. The image is a mirror image of the original figure.

Practice drawing a figure and its reflection.

The result of giving an object a reflection in a line of symmetry is called its **mirror image.**

Turning a figure around a point is called a rotation. For example, a windmill rotates around a center axis. Each vane moves through an angle of equal degrees.

Rotate the arrow (→) 90° to the right by the number of turns listed below:

→   1 turn to the right   ↓

→   2 turns to the right   ←

→   3 turns to the right   ↑

→   4 turns to the right   →

Rotate the figure below to the right by the number of turns listed.

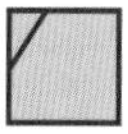

1 turn to the right

2 turns to the right

3 turns to the right

4 turns to the right

A **rotation** is a transformation in which every point of an object turns through the same angle around a common center.

The figures below are examples of rotations.

1.

2.

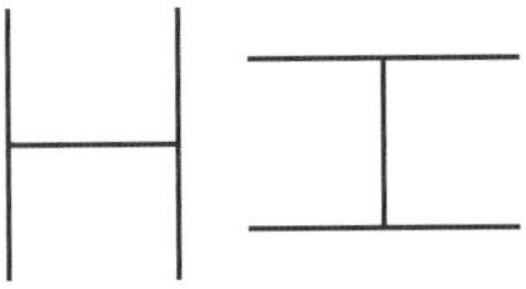

Flip the figure below and rotate it one turn to the left.

| original | flip | rotate |
|----------|------|--------|

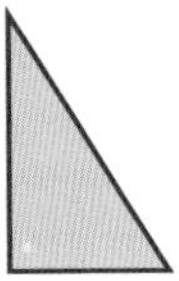

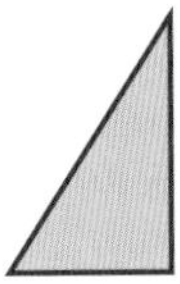

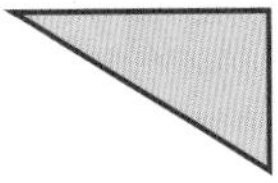

Slide the rectangle and then rotate it one turn to the right.

original

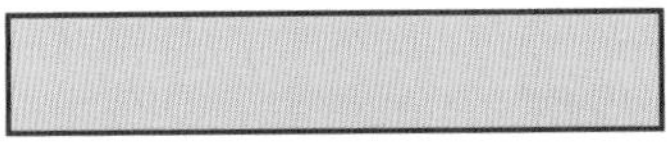

slide

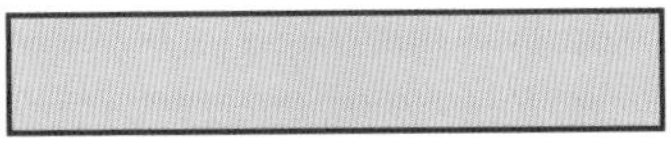

rotate

A **slide** moves a figure up, down, or over.
A **flip** produces a mirror image of a figure.
A **turn** rotates a figure around a point.

Boxes are sold to companies as two-dimensional patterns. Then they are put together to make the shape of the three-dimensional figure. Shipping empty containers as two-dimensional objects saves lots of room on delivery trucks, which saves lots of money.

Each of the patterns below can be folded to make a cube.

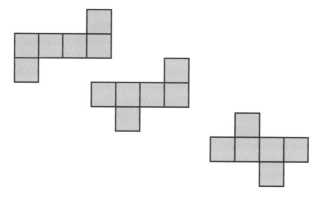

Practice folding the patterns. Place letters in the squares to help you fold it into a cube.

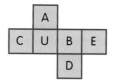

Fold the pattern.

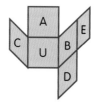

A **cube** is a solid with all its faces square and all its edges equal in length. The shape of a die is a cube.

Here is a pattern for a hexagonal prism.

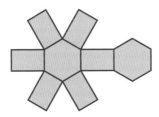

This is a pattern for a cylinder.

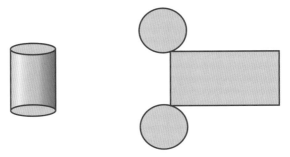

**How do you draw a picture of a cube or other prism?**

**Step 1:** Draw a base.

**Step 2:** Draw a second equal base.

**Step 3:** Draw lines to connect the bases as their vertices.

Make up a pattern for a three-dimensional figure, then try to fold your pattern to make the three-dimensional object.

The perimeter of a figure is the distance around it. To find the perimeter of a polygon, add the lengths of all the sides.

Find the perimeter of this figure. Let P = perimeter.

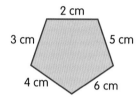

Add the lengths of all the sides.

$$P = 3 \text{ cm} + 2 \text{ cm} + 5 \text{ cm} + 6 \text{ cm} + 4 \text{ cm}$$
$$P = 20 \text{ cm}$$

## Perimeter of a Square

A square is a polygon that has four equal sides. You can use a formula to find the perimeter of a square. The perimeter is equal to s + s + s + s, or four times the side.

**Perimeter of a square**

$$P = 4 \times s$$

**Find the perimeter of the square.**

**Step 1:** Write the formula.

3 cm

$$P = 4 \times s$$

**Step 2:** Solve for P.

$$P = 4 \times 3 \text{ cm}$$
$$P = 12 \text{ cm}$$

A **polygon** is a closed figure bounded by line segments.
**Perimeter of a polygon** = the sum of all the sides.
**Perimeter of a square** = 4 x s, where s = length of one side.

# Perimeter of a Rectangle

A rectangle is a polygon that has four sides. Opposite sides of a rectangle are congruent. You can use a formula to find the perimeter of a rectangle. The perimeter is equal to 2 times the length plus 2 times the width.

**Perimeter of a rectangle**

$$P = (2 \times \ell) + (2 \times w)$$

**Find the perimeter of the rectangle.**

6 m

4 m

**Step 1:** Write the formula. $P = (2 \times \ell) + (2 \times w)$

**Step 2:** Multiply. $P = (2 \times 6 \text{ m}) + (2 \times 4 \text{ m})$
$P = 12 \text{ m} + 8 \text{ m}$

**Step 3:** Add. $P = 20 \text{ m}$

# Perimeter of a Triangle

To find the perimeter of a triangle, add the lengths of the sides.

Find the perimeter of a triangle.

5 ft     7 ft

4 ft

Add the lengths of the sides. $P = 5 \text{ ft} + 4 \text{ ft} + 7 \text{ ft}$

$P = 16 \text{ ft}$

Find the perimeter of each room in your home. What room has the largest perimeter?

Perimeter of a rectangle $= (2 \times \ell) + (2 \times w)$.

Your parents are going to carpet your living room. They must know the length and width of the room before they go to the store. That way they will know the area of the room and how much carpet to purchase.

### Area of a Rectangle

Area is the number of square units needed to cover a certain region. If the small square below is one unit of area, how many units are there in this rectangle?

☐ = 1 square unit

The area of a rectangle can be found by multiplying length by width. This rectangle has 3 rows of 4 squares. $3 \times 4 = 12$. The area of the rectangle is 12 square units. Count the squares to check your answer.

Find the area of this rectangle.

There are 2 rows of 6 squares and 1 row of 6 half squares.

Find the total square units.

| | |
|---|---|
| 2 rows of 6 squares | $2 \times 6 = \quad 12$ |
| 1 row of 6 half squares | $1 \times 6 \times \dfrac{1}{2} = \dfrac{+\ 3}{15}$ |

The area of the rectangle is 15 square units.

---

**Area of a rectangle** = length × width, or $\ell w$.

Suppose your living room has a length of 12 feet and a width of 10 feet. What is the area of the room?

**Step 1:** Write the formula.

Area = length × width, or
$$A = \ell \times w$$

**Step 2:** Solve for A.

$$A = 12 \text{ ft} \times 10 \text{ ft}$$
$$A = 120 \text{ square feet}$$

The area of the room is 120 square feet. The units for area are always square units.

## Area of a Square

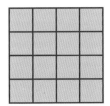

**Area of a square**
$$A = s \times s, \text{ or } A = s^2.$$

To find the area, square the side.

Use the formula to find the area of the above square.

$$A = s \times s$$
$$A = 4 \times 4$$
$$A = 16 \text{ square units}$$

*Find the area of each room in your home. Which room has the largest area?*

**Area of a square** = side × side, or s × s, or $s^2$.

Many home improvement projects, such as wallpapering, involve figuring out areas. Many rooms are not in the shape of a rectangle or square. Some rooms have an irregular shape, and homeowners must understand how to find the area of triangles to get an accurate area measurement.

## Area of a Triangle

Find the area of the triangle.

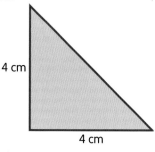

4 cm

4 cm

You can find the area of this triangle by placing it on a grid.

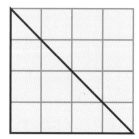

Count the square units the triangle covers.

How many whole square units does the triangle cover?

$\square$ = 6 square units

How many one half square units does the triangle cover?

$\triangle$ = 4 half or 2 whole square units

Area = 6 square units + 2 square units

The area of the triangle is 8 square units, or 8 square cm.

---

**area** — The number of square units in a surface.

You can use a formula to find the area of a triangle. The area is equal to one half the base times the height.

**Area of a triangle**

$$A = \frac{1}{2} \times b \times h$$

**Find the area of the triangle.**

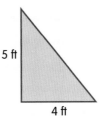

5 ft

4 ft

**Step 1:** Write the formula.
Identify the base and height.

$$A = \frac{1}{2} \times b \times h$$

**Step 2:** Multiply. $\frac{1}{2}$ of 4 ft is 2 ft.

$$A = \frac{1}{2} \times 4 \text{ ft} \times 5 \text{ ft}$$

$$A = 2 \text{ ft} \times 5 \text{ ft}$$

$$A = 10 \text{ sq ft}$$

The area is 10 square feet.

Practice finding the area of triangles. Have a friend draw different triangles. Find the area using a grid and then the formula $\frac{1}{2} \times b \times h$.

Area of a triangle $= \frac{1}{2} \times$ base $\times$ height.

Tiles for a floor have to fit together without gaps between them. Most people use square tiles, but what if you used other shapes such as parallelograms to cover the floor of a room? How would you figure out how many to buy to cover the area of floor being tiled?

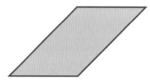

Find the area of the parallelogram. Use graph paper. Use each small square as one square unit of area.

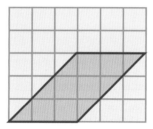

Count the square units the parallelogram covers.

How many whole square units does the parallelogram cover?

☐ = 6 square units

How many one-half square units does the parallelogram cover?

◺ = 6 half square units, or 3 square units

Add:      Area = 6 square units + 3 square units
             Area = 9 square units

The area of the parallelogram is 9 square units.

A **parallelogram** is a quadrilateral with two pairs of parallel sides.

You can use a formula to find the area of a parallelogram. The area is equal to the base times the height.

**Area of a parallelogram**

$$A = b \times h$$

**Find the area of the parallelogram.**

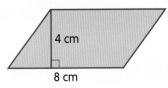

4 cm

8 cm

**Step 1:** Write the formula. Identify the base and height.

$A = b \times h$

base = 8 cm

height = 4 cm

**Step 2:** Multiply.

$A = 8 \text{ cm} \times 4 \text{ cm}$

$A = 32 \text{ sq cm}$

The area of the parallelogram is 32 square centimeters.

## Parallelograms and Triangles

Find the area of the same parallelogram by dividing it into two equal triangles.

Find the sum of the areas of the triangles.

$A = (\frac{1}{2} \times b \times h) + (\frac{1}{2} \times b \times h)$

$A = (\frac{1}{2} \times 8 \text{ cm} \times 4 \text{ cm}) + (\frac{1}{2} \times 8 \text{ cm} \times 4 \text{ cm})$

$A = 16 + 16 = 32 \text{ sq cm}$

4 cm

8 cm

Practice finding the area of a parallelogram by using graph paper, dividing it into two triangles, and using the formula.

**Area of a parallelogram** = base × height, or b × h.
**Square centimeters** can be abbreviated as **sq cm**.

Find a round pizza pan, a saucer, and a dinner plate. Which of them has the greatest circumference and area?

## Circumference of a Circle

The circumference of a circle is another name for the perimeter of a circle. It is the distance around the circle. Suppose your dinner plate had a diameter of 8 inches. What is the circumference of the plate?

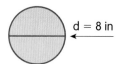

circumference of a circle

$$c = \pi \times d$$

About 2500 years ago it was proven that the circumference divided by the diameter is the same number, or a constant, for every circle. This value is called *pi* and is represented by the Greek letter $\pi$. The value of pi cannot be represented by an exact number. The most common approximation used for pi is 3.14, or $\frac{22}{7}$.

---

**Find the circumference of the dinner plate.**

**Step 1:** Write the formula for circumference.      $C = \pi \times d$

**Step 2:** Multiply.

$$
\begin{array}{r}
C = 3.14 \times 8 \text{ in} \\
3.14 \\
\times\ 8 \text{ in} \\
\hline
25.12 \text{ in}
\end{array}
$$

The circumference of the dinner plate is 25.12 in.

---

**circumference** — The distance around the outside of a circle, also called the perimeter.
**Circumference of a circle** = $\pi \times d$.

# Area of a Circle

To find the area of a circle, multiply π by the square of the radius.

**Area of a circle**

$$A = \pi \times r \times r$$

**or**

$$A = \pi r^2$$

---

**Find the area of the dinner plate. The diameter of the plate is 8 inches. The radius is half the diameter.**

d = 8 in

r = 4 in

$$r = \frac{d}{2}$$

$$r = \frac{8 \text{ in}}{2}$$

$$r = 4 \text{ in}$$

**Step 1:** Write the formula.

$$A = \pi \times r \times r$$

**Step 2:** Multiply.

$$A = 3.14 \times 4 \text{ in} \times 4 \text{ in}$$

```
        3.14
      × 4 in
     12.56 in
      × 4 in
   50.24 sq in
```

The area of the dinner plate is 50.24 square inches.

---

Now find the circumference and area of the pizza pan and saucer. In square units, what would be the area of a pizza baked on the pan? How many dinner plates could you fill with the pizza? How many saucers?

---

**Area of a circle** = π × radius × radius, or $\pi r^2$.

Suppose you wanted to help your parents put new heatproof plastic on a countertop with the following shape. How many square feet of plastic should you buy?

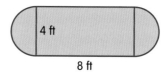

A composite is a figure made up of distinct parts. This figure is an example of a composite. It is made up of different parts. It has two half circles and one rectangle. You can divide the countertop into three regions and find the area of each section.

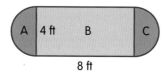

The area of the countertop is equal to the sum of the areas of A, B, and C.

$$Area = area\ A + area\ B + area\ C$$

Section A and section C are both half circles, or semicircles, with a diameter of 4 ft. The area of A is the same as the area of C.

### Area of a semicircle

$$A = \frac{1}{2} \pi r^2$$

Section B is a rectangle.

### Area of a rectangle

$$A = \ell w$$

---

**Area of a semicircle** $= \frac{1}{2} \times \pi \times$ radius $\times$ radius, or $\frac{1}{2} \pi r^2$.

**Area of a rectangle** $=$ length $\times$ width, or $\ell w$.

**Find the area of A.**

**Step 1:** Write the formula.

$$A = \frac{1}{2} \times \pi \times r \times r$$

**Step 2:** Find the radius.

$$r = \frac{d}{2} = \frac{4 \text{ ft}}{2} = 2 \text{ ft}$$

**Step 3:** Multiply.

$$A = \frac{1}{2} \times 3.14 \times 2 \text{ ft} \times 2 \text{ ft}$$
$$A = 6.28 \text{ sq ft}$$

The area of A is 6.28 sq ft.

**Find the area of B.**

**Step 1:** Write the formula.

$$A = \ell \times w$$

**Step 2:** Multiply.

$$A = 8 \text{ ft} \times 4 \text{ ft}$$
$$A = 32 \text{ sq ft}$$

The area of B is 32 sq ft.

**Find the area of C.**

Area of A = area of C, so the area of C = 6.28 sq ft.

Find the area of the countertop.

Area = area A + area B + area C
Area = 6.28 sq ft + 32 sq ft + 6.28 sq ft
Area = 44.56 sq ft

You need 44.56 square feet of plastic to cover the countertop.

Find an example of a composite in your home. What different shapes are in your composite?

Space has three dimensions: length, width, and height. The amount that a three-dimensional figure can hold is called its volume. Since it involves three dimensions, volume is measured in cubic units. Some common units of volume are cubic inches, cubic feet, cubic yards, cubic centimeters, and cubic meters.

How many 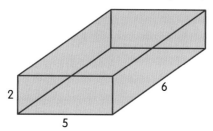 (cubes) are needed to fill the rectangular prism?

Fill in the first layer.

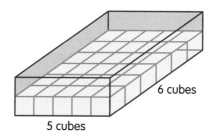

6 cubes

5 cubes

1 layer = 5 × 6 cubes
1 layer = 30 cubes

How many cubes will make two layers?

2 layers = 2 × 5 × 6
2 layers = 60 cubes

It will take 60 cubes to fill the rectangular prism.

**prism** — A solid, three-dimensional shape with flat sides.
To review prisms, see pages 20–21.

You can use a formula to find the volume of a prism. The volume is equal to the area of the base times the height.

**Volume of a prism**
V = area of base × height

Find the volume of the rectangular prism.

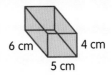

6 cm    4 cm
5 cm

**Step 1:** Find the area of the base.

**Area of a Rectangle**    6 cm
A = ℓ × w                      5 cm
A = 5 cm × 6 cm
A = 30 sq cm

The area of the base is 30 sq cm.

**Step 2:** Find the volume.

Volume = area of base × height
V = 30 sq cm × 4 cm
V = 120 cubic cm

The volume of the rectangular prism is 120 cubic cm.

Find the volume of a shoe box or the box of your favorite cereal.

**Volume of a prism** = area of base × height.

To find the volume of a cone, multiply $\frac{1}{3}$ times the area of the base times the height. Remember the area of a circular base = $\pi r^2$.

**Volume of a cone**

$V = \frac{1}{3} \pi r^2 h$      or      $V = \frac{1}{3} \times \pi \times r^2 \times h$

$V$ = volume      $\pi = \frac{22}{7}$      $r$ = radius      $h$ = height

---

**Find the volume of the cone.**

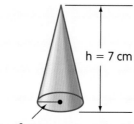

h = 7 cm

r = 3 cm

To find $r^2$, multiply $3 \times 3$; $r^2 = 9$

**Step 1:** Write the formula.      $V = \frac{1}{3} \pi r^2 h$

**Step 2:** Rewrite formula using the values for $\pi$, $r^2$, and $h$.      $V = \frac{1}{3} \times \frac{22}{7} \times \frac{9}{1} \times \frac{7}{1}$

**Step 3:** Reduce before multiplying.      $V = \frac{1}{\cancel{3}} \times \frac{22}{\cancel{7}} \times \frac{\cancel{9}^3}{1} \times \frac{\cancel{7}^1}{1}$

**Step 4:** Multiply.      $V = 1 \times 22 \times 3 = 66$

The volume of the cone is 66 cubic centimeters, or 66 cu cm, or 66 cm³.

---

**Volume of a cone** $= \frac{1}{3} \pi r^2 h$.

# Volume of Cylinders

To find the volume of a cylinder, multiply the area of the base by the height.

**Volume of a cylinder**
V = area of base × height
area of base = area of a circle = $\pi r^2$
V = $\pi r^2 h$, or V = $\pi \times r \times r \times h$

**Find the volume of the cylinder.**

r = 6 cm $\longrightarrow$ 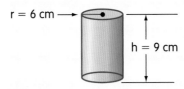 h = 9 cm

**Step 1:** Write the formula

$V = \pi \times r \times r \times h$

**Step 2:** Rewrite formula using the values for $\pi$, r, and h.

$V = 3.14 \times 6 \times 6 \times 9$

**Step 3:** Multiply.

$$
\begin{array}{ccc}
3.14 & 18.84 & 113.04 \\
\times\, 6 & \times\, 6 & \times\, 9 \\
\hline
18.84 & 113.04 & 1017.36
\end{array}
$$

The volume of the cylinder is 1017.36 cubic cm.

Make a list of items that are shaped like a cone or a cylinder. Can you find their volumes?

Volume of a cylinder = area of base × height.
$\pi$ = **3.14**

# Further Reading

## Books

Learning Express Editors. *Geometry Success in 20 Minutes a Day (Skill Builders)*. New York: Learning Express, LLC. 2010

Leff, Lawrence S. *E-Z Geometry*. New York: Barron's Educational Series, Inc., 2009.

Ryan, Mark. *Geometry For Dummies*. New Jersey: Wiley Publishing Inc., 2008.

## Internet Addresses

Education for Kids, Inc. Flashcards for Kids. ©1995–2005. <http://www.edu4kids.com/index.php?TB=2&page=12>.

Math2.org. ©1995–2003. <http://www.math2.org/>.

The Math Forum. *Ask Dr. Math*. © 1994–2000. <http://mathforum.org/dr.math/>.

Mrs. Glosser's Math Goodies, Inc. *Mrs. Glosser's Math Goodies*. © 1999–2000. <http://www.mathgoodies.com>.

Webmath. n.d. <http://www.webmath.com/index5.html>.